This book belongs to

. . . .

Reading with your child

Tips for sharing this book

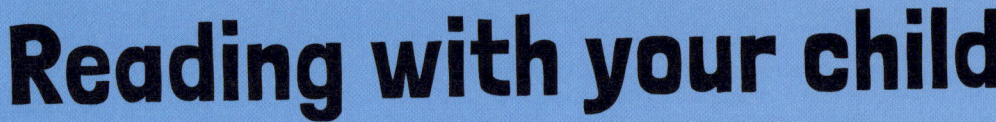

Look at the front cover. What does your child think might happen in the story?

Talk about the back cover blurb. Why might it be difficult for a mouse to reach a cake that is on top of a cupboard?

During reading

- Encourage your child to describe what is going on in the pictures.

- Ask your child what is happening, and what they think might happen next.

- When you turn the page to see what actually happens, the outcome may or may not be what you expect! Talk about it.

- Give them lots of praise as you go along!

After reading

- Look at the back for some fun activities.

OXFORD
UNIVERSITY PRESS

Great Clarendon Street, Oxford OX2 6DP
Oxford University Press is a department of the University of Oxford.
It furthers the University's objective of excellence in research, scholarship,
and education by publishing worldwide. Oxford is a registered trade mark
of Oxford University Press in the UK and in certain other countries

British Library Cataloguing in Publication Data

Data available
ISBN: 978-0-19-278280-9

1 3 5 7 9 10 8 6 4 2

Printed in China

Paper used in the production of this book is a natural,
recyclable product made from wood grown in sustainable
forests. The manufacturing process conforms to the
environmentalbregulations of the country of origin.

TONY NEAL

HOP ON TOP, MOUSE!

OXFORD

UNIVERSITY PRESS

EAT ME!

Yum!

Too high!

Help!

EAT ME!

Too slippery!

EAT ME!

Come and help, Rabbit!

We are too short!

I have a plan!

EAT ME!

Let's work
TOGETHER!

EAT ME!

Still too far!

EAT ME!

Up you come!

Climb up,
frog!

Hop on top,
Mouse!

So close . . .

Wobble,
wobble!

My cake.

OUR

cake.

Activities

Height

The tallest toy

Ask your child to find their favourite toy.

Now ask them to find a toy that is **taller**, and a toy that is **shorter**.

Can they put the toys in order, from **shortest** to **tallest**?

High and low walk

While on a walk with your child ask them to list three things they can see that are high, and three that are low.

What is the tallest thing that they can see?

Vocabulary:

tall
taller
tallest
high
up

short
shorter
shortest
low
down